Unequal

Unequally Yoked

Five Steps to Living Victoriously
While In the Valley

Kaye Edwards

Leeway Publishers
Published by Leeway Artisans
PO Box 1577, Laurel, MD 20707
www.LeewayArtisans.com

Edited by Kay Coulter
Book & Cover Design by Mykle A. Lee

ISBN: 0-9744929-3-0

Library of Congress Control Number: 2005923010

First Edition
Printed in the United States of America

Table of Contents

Introduction

Final Thoughts

Dedication and Thank Yous

Although this book is geared towards those who are unequally yoked, it is dedicated to each of my children – Tanisha, Toni and my son, Renardo, as I would not have any of them unequally yoked.

I also dedicate this book to the young women and men in my life that I have watched grow up who have either recently graduated high school or will be doing so in the near future. It is my prayer that none of these young people would become unequally yoked.

First, I want to thank God. It's because of his grace and mercy that I am even here to tell a story; my pastor Irving J. Clark II and his wife Toni – I cannot begin to list the many things for which I am thankful for when it comes to you guys. Just know that I am, in part, because of you; and the members of my former church, Bethel Bible for allowing me to share my poetry with the congregation on Sunday mornings, for cheering me on and believing in me. I also want to thank those members in my current church home who have prayed for me and encouraged me in this endeavor, and to my mother for always believing that I could do and be anything I put my mind to.

And I also want to thank those friends and co-workers who have encouraged me and have prayed for me through the years. I hope you know who you are.

I love you all!

Introduction

"Be ye not unequally yoked together with unbelievers: for what fellowship hath righteousness with unrighteousness? and what communion hath light with darkness?" 2 Corinthians 6:14

*M*y name is Kaye Edwards. I am the mother of three and have been married for over 14 years to a man that has not accepted Christ as his Savior. And if you are like me, at times I have needed someone to talk to who could truly relate to what I go through—the emptiness, the constant warfare and loneliness. Being "unequally yoked" is a lesson in longsuffering that I could have done without (but maybe there's a purpose). Whoever said, "sin in haste, repent in leisure" never lied. For there are consequences for every choice made under the Son/sun.

This book is to provide encouragement and a process of healing for those many, many women and men who are unequally yoked (I do not speak to those who were married while both were unsaved. I believe that the Lord deals with those cases in a totally different manner, as the two unsaved souls did not marry in disobedience to God's Word). Whether by blatant disobedience or omission, the results are the same. Somewhere along the line we lost faith and in the time that it took the eye to blink, we took our eyes off of God and gave Satan the toehold he needed to cause us to stumble. And we now find ourselves on a journey that is both difficult and often lonely. And yet you can bear all sorts of good fruit, if you allow the Lord to lead, confess your sin, forgive yourself and allow God to do a good work.

Having been on this journey for some time, it is my hope that I can offer some of the bits of wisdom I have learned along the way. It is my prayer that this book will provide some words of support when days seem to be at their darkest. I know there are thousands out there who could use some words that might help to make the weight feel lighter, and most importantly, help them realize that they are not alone, and know that with faith and belief in God and His word, *we* can live victorious lives even with our unsaved spouses.

My experience has led me to believe that there are five basic steps that can help you to live a more victorious life and heal your heart and mind as you walk a path that is seemingly impossible!

The first step involves reflection on your life at the time you made the fateful error in judgment. After some honest evaluation, accept the fact that the fault lies with you and no one else.

Next, you need to seek God's forgiveness immediately. Waiting to do so is almost certain to be a detriment to your mental well-being. After you ask and receive God's forgiveness, forgive yourself, which is the next step. Let go of the hurt and disappointment that you have in you. Ask God to help you forgive you!

Also, we have to realize that every choice comes with corresponding consequences. Some are easier to bear than others, and unfortunately, we neither get to pick our consequences, nor do we have the luxury of choosing either the weight or length of time we must bear them. Therefore, we must learn to stand strong while in the valley.

In addition, we have to learn to tame our tongues. At the very least, we must work on how we speak to our spouses, and be cognizant of the things said into their hearing. The way we talk to our spouses could have a direct affect on whether they come to a saving knowledge of Jesus Christ. Therefore, we must learn to temper our words with a grain of salt.

Finally, you have to realize that disobedience and poor choices doesn't mean that God can't or won't use you. You still have the freedom to find out God's will and purpose for your life and work on fulfilling that.

To close out, I have dedicated the last chapter specifically to women who are about to make the same mistake. Some have been fighting it, but because their trust and focus is no longer God directed, they continue to lean ever closer towards becoming unequally yoked. It is my earnest prayer that after reading this book, minds and hearts are changed when it comes to considering being unequally yoked.

Chapter 1
How Did You Get Here?

"*H*ow did you get here, nobody's supposed to be here?" Those are words from a song by a R&B artist *(Deborah Cox, One Wish, 1999).* While the rest of the words of the song aren't applicable, these words came to mind when I thought about how I ended up on this particular journey. Because as God's children, we have no business here, in marriages to unsaved partners, and the question is, "How did we get here?" My prayer is that we find out the answer to that question, and pass along the knowledge to others who find themselves considering this same choice.

How did we get here?

The answer is simple and may be hard to accept. In a word, sin. That's right! We took our eyes off God. We lost faith and stopped believing, if only for a minute. It was just enough time for

Satan to gain enough ground to plant the seed(s) necessary to make us believe it was okay to make a serious move that was contrary to God's Word and his will.

By not staying in prayer and God's Word, and/or going places and doing things that you may have had the freedom to do, but were spiritually fruitless, you became an easier target. I say easier, because you became a target the day you accepted Christ as your personal Savior.

Satan may not be able to take your salvation, but he can make you an ineffective witness for Christ. He wants you to be the kind of witness that helps to advance *his* kingdom. Though not intentionally on your part, disobedience helps his cause. That is why I say sin is how you got here. Your focus momentarily left Christ and just that small moment in time, was all the enemy needed to start a work in you—making you feel insecure due to maybe finances, health, age, your physical appearance or loneliness. Whatever it was, Satan knew exactly where to have you focus your doubts. He figured out your vulnerable spot and he jumped all over it. A shift in focus made it easier for the enemy to deceive.

With your focus shifted, you were ripe for the pickin' and it was just what Satan was counting on when tall, dark and unsaved popped into your life. Men, remember how despite the fact that the she was neither saved, nor did she honestly appear to be all that interested in the things of God, you decided that she was "the one?" And ladies, even though you knew he was a little rough around the edges, you thought you could change him, right? So you just hoped that with all the good qualities and good intentions that they seemed to possess (I say "seem" because without Jesus it's all an illusion), along with the changes you could help with, that surely everything would turn out all right. The end result, you chose to ignore those nagging voices that were screaming, "Don't go there!"

The Warning Signs

As a true Christian, you probably received a lot of those nagging doubts, or should I call them warning signals. Let's go back to when you were being pursued. How many times were you asked, "Do they know Jesus? What's their personal testimony? Are you sure you want to do this?" How many times did you realize that the two of you never prayed together or even really discussed the Bible or anything scriptural? How consistent was their attendance at church? Were they a working member of the church or more of pew warmer? How fast was their exit after the benediction? Did they even stay until then? Here's the biggie— were you sleeping together prior to marriage?!

Ladies and gentlemen, do not kid yourselves, having sex with someone prior to marriage is wrong and not in God's will. His Word clearly states his views on all sexual behavior outside the confines of marriage. I know it's the 21st Century, but it's still a

[13b]Now the body is not for sexual immorality but for the Lord, and the Lord for the body. [18]Flee sexual immorality. Every sin that a man does is outside the body, but he who commits sexual immorality sins against his own body. [19]Or do you not know that your body is the temple of the Holy Spirit who is in you, whom you have from God, and you are not your own? [20]For you were bought at a price; therefore glorify God in your body and in your spirit, which are God's.

- I Corinthians 6:13b, 18-20 (NKJV)

sin and it is still unacceptable to the Father. God's Word does not change.

If we just took some time to think about it, sex prior to marriage isn't a wise course of action. From a woman's perspective, we for the most part are built differently. Our emotions play a large part in our decision-making, and sex comes with a lot of emotional issues that can and do cloud one's judgment. We all know that hormones can be a beast, but just because the two of you lust well together does not mean that you have anything else in common. Remove the sex factor and it gives you and your potential spouse time to truly get to know each other. And you owe it to yourself to know that sex is not the only reason you two hit it off. Oftentimes we confuse lust with love and they are not the same. If you can't talk to each other out of the bedroom, your marriage will be like a prison term. You'll end up just waiting for your "sentence" to end.

Having other shared common interests is very important, as the day could come when you two may not be able to have marital relations for long periods of time, if ever again! Life happens! Take the time to develop a true and solid friendship. Consider the words in marriage vows, "till death do you part." You will spend the rest of your life with this person. Your relationship before marriage should be considered time well invested to be sure of God's will. Even if it takes a year or two or three, etc. A man or woman who claims to be saved and sold out for Jesus has no business crossing that line or trying to encourage you to do so. If you tell them no when they first try and they persist after every date, you have been duly warned. They are neither taking their walk with the Lord nor your stand on premarital sex seriously. Feel free to give them the benefit of the doubt just once, in case they are actually testing your claim of walking upright with God (it only qualifies as a test, if they turn you down, and sex no longer is a constant source of conversation).

If you were attending a church that didn't give you a watered down version of the Word, you received even more flashing red lights! Here's one—would your pastor do the ceremony? Did you two have pre-marital counseling? If you have mentors or friends that are serious about their walk with God, then somewhere along the way you got those warning signals in many forms. You may have received them in the form of questions from friends, family and/or sermons! I know from experience that sermons are real good at convicting you of sin, especially when you think you are the only one who knows what's happening! When it feels like every word the preacher says is directed at you, or if it sounds like your best friend has told the pastor all your business, that was God talking to you via the pastor, but again you closed your ears. You brushed off the warning signs and boldly said, "I do" to living a life of semi-darkness.

Honest Conclusion: It was Disobedience

> [14]Do not be joined together with those who do not belong to Christ. How can that which is good get along with that which is bad? How can light be in the same place with darkness?
>
> -2 Corinthians 6:14 (NLV)

As God's elect, we are of the light and what fellowship hath light with darkness. I didn't say it, God said it. So don't shoot the messenger! These are truths that I also had to deal with. I had to

9

accept the fact that I put myself here—not God and not the man that I so ignorantly married. It was my responsibility to pray and to wait on what *His* will was for me. If it had taken a year or even 10 years, I was supposed to wait on the Lord. Isaiah 40:31 tells us to wait on the Lord, and that if we wait, God will renew our strength. That is why it is so important to read the Bible and pray on a daily basis, so that you can stay tuned to the Father. You can't stay tuned if you don't keep in touch.

Psalm 119:11
"Thy word have I hid in mine heart
that I might not sin against thee."

As I come to the end of this chapter, I thought it important to break down the reasons why I felt it was so important to know how you got here in the first place. The reason is two-fold. One, your spouse could walk out on you and it's my belief from the Word, I Corinthians 7:15, that we are not held to account in such cases, which leaves you free to marry again (be mindful, it has to be the unsaved spouse's desire to leave the marriage, without any help from you, for that too would have its own consequences); and two, your spouse could simply pass away. Under those circumstances, you do not want to repeat the same error in judgment should you find yourself again thinking to marry. God may not allow such merciful outs the second time around. Not saying that God would be the one responsible for your spouse either leaving or dying, but he definitely can step in and allow not only longevity of life, but he can put it in the heart of the next spouse to stay!

In either case, I am thinking to repeat the same mistake could be even more costly than the first. That is why it is important to know what your mindset was during the period of time in your life when you opted to marry out of God's will. To know what was going on that caused you to put down your guard. There may be some unfinished baggage from your past that has made it hard for you to discern. There are all sorts of trauma you may have encountered in life that can make making good judgments almost impossible. We have to let go of old hurts and fears before we can be a productive part of any intimate relationship. Was there rape, molestation, abuse by parent or spouse? Were you abandoned? These are just a few things left unresolved that have a way of messing with your life in the present. Knowing the root of your previous circumstances may help you not to repeat the same mistake(s).

Once you have acknowledged honestly how you got where you are, it is time to find ways to live where you are that would be pleasing to God. And it will not be easy. It is not easy living with someone that is not going in the opposite direction as you are spiritually. There is serious warfare going on in your home, and whether or not you survive depends on your faith in God. You will need all the faith of Abraham or at least a portion of it to survive an indeterminate number of years of your life in an added battlefield of your own making (added because as God's elect, we are already on the battlefield).

Fact: there is no guarantee that your spouse will come to salvation. In other words, you have to find a way to live with your choice. The success or failure in how you handle things within the marriage will depend on you. It will depend on your personal relationship with God. I urge you to develop a one-on-one with God, and to nurture it by talking with God daily through prayer and by reading His Word. It is my sincere hope that the tools herein will help you on this journey, as they have and are helping me.

I am ending this chapter with a poem entitled "Deceived." I wrote this one day as I reflected on how I got here. The poem summed up the step by step accounting of how I came to be unequally yoked.

STEP ONE: *Reflect on your life and come to the honest conclusion that you got "here" because of disobedience to God.*

Reflection: What were the warning signs that you ignored in the beginning before you came to marry an unsaved partner?

Did you know that you were walking the path of disobedience when you involved yourself with this person?

Might there have been any old hurts or fears that caused you to pursue your spouse despite the knowledge of it being disobedient to God?

Were there people you could talk with, such as a pastor, prayer partner, etc. about the danger of an unequally yoked relationship?

Do you now acknowledge the fact that you ignored the warning signs and pursued disobedience?

Discussion: These reflections may bring up old hurts and shames, but again it is vital to get to the root of the disobedience, and recognize your situation evolved from sin. Fully understanding the cause will equip you with better vision for yourself as well as for others in danger of making the same mistake.

Take time and reflect on 2 Corinthians 6:14 because it is important to know exactly what type of situation you know live with. And, as I will explain in the next chapter, you will need to know this as sin so that you can bring it to God.

Deceived

He said he wanted a family that
Went to church and prayed together.
To establish a bond that could withstand
The stormy weather.

Whatever you were looking for, somehow
He was too.
That was your first signal that it may be
Too good to be true.

Before the marriage he went to church, as he, like
You were trying to change his "backslidden" ways
It was never a question where he would be
On any given Sunday.

You said, "I do," and shortly after the
Truth hit the fan, so to speak.
The man of your dreams was no knight in
Shining armor, he was a lying sneak.

Why didn't you truly seek God's counsel
Before you made such a serious move?
Why didn't you realize that you had so
Very much to lose?

A living hell you now live, due to a lack of
Faith and your unbelief.
You've landed in a river of unhappiness

And constant, heartbreaking grief.

Lightness and darkness are at opposition;
Therefore the two are not to mix.
The Word of God was very clear when it
Commanded and spoke of this.

Chapter II
The Importance of Forgiveness

*N*ow that you have acknowledged your sin, the next step is to ask the Father to forgive you. The Bible tells us in 1 John 1:9: *"If we confess our sins, he is faithful and just to forgive us our sins, and to cleanse us from all unrighteousness."* It is not that God doesn't know what you've done, but he wants you to acknowledge your own sins. He wants you to truly repent, turn from your wicked ways and he will remember your sin no more.

I believe that personal acknowledgement helps one to see their sin for what it is. In a way, it's like if we don't say it, it's not true. That is why the confession of sin is so important. I find verbal acknowledgement helps me to see and accept the truth of my actions. Once the words are said out loud and I hear them, it seems to add a new perspective, and it helps take me out of denial.

Confession = Freedom

God's forgiveness of our sins does not mean that there are no consequences to be had, but we will hold the subject of consequences for later. Let's talk about our forgiving Father. God's forgiveness releases us from any hold that sin has on us. Hence the importance of confessing and believing in your heart that God has forgiven you. If not, that sin becomes the winner because you are still under bondage. If you allow it, unconfessed sin will rule your life so to speak. It can and will sap the joy right out of your life.

> [22] I love God's law with all my heart. [23] But there is another law at work within me that is at war with my mind. This law wins the fight and makes me a slave to the sin that is still within me. [24] Oh, what a miserable person I am! Who will free me from this life that is dominated by sin? [25] Thank God! The answer is in Jesus Christ our Lord.
>
> - Romans 7:22-25 (NLT)

When you fail to seek God's forgiveness, guilt will just gnaw and gnaw at you until you either finally go to God seeking forgiveness or you fall further into disobedience. For instance, it is possible to find yourself avoiding church all together in order to avoid the conviction that comes from hearing God's Word. If you start avoiding church or related activities, or people from church; it is a good indication that you may be under bondage to unconfessed sin. And sin that is not confessed is disobedience, which is bad enough, but unchecked, it can lead to more sin. When we don't pray and ask God for his forgiveness, it leaves that sin eating at us, leading to more possible acts of disobedience, all because we failed to seek

18

the Lord's forgiveness. Confession is very important in the life of a believer, as it is what God commands us to do when we sin, because after confession comes divine forgiveness, which is important if we are to be in fellowship with God. Forgiveness is the very reason any one of us will even see Heaven someday, which further illustrates how important God's forgiveness is when we fall out of fellowship with Him.

Unconfessed sin takes us out of fellowship with the Father. Fellowship with Christ is essential for the positive growth in the life of the believer, ergo unconfessed sin puts up a wall between us and God, and with a wall up, we miss blessings, and other prayers may go unanswered. It is very important to keep our hearts and minds right with God. The Lord has given us an avenue of escape, and we find it through prayer. In order to move on in your life, constant confession of sin is necessary and it is balm for the spirit. So no matter the sin, always, always go to God, ask Him to forgive you and release yourself from the negative fallout that will result if your sins go unconfessed.

> [4] Day and night your hand of discipline was heavy on me. My strength evaporated like water in the summer heat. [5] Finally, I confessed all my sins to you and stopped trying to hide them. I said to myself, "I will confess my rebellion to the LORD." And you forgave me! All my guilt is gone.
> [6] Therefore, let all the godly confess their rebellion to you while there is time, that they may not drown in the floodwaters of judgment.
> - Psalms 32:4-6 (NLT)

Forgiving Yourself

This brings us to another area of forgiveness—forgiving yourself! Depending on how deep the offense, this is truly something that is not easy to do. After you receive God's forgiveness, you have to do the same for yourself. To some this may sound easy, but it is not. I could not forgive myself for years! I could not get over disappointing God yet again; for making a decision that affected my life negatively in so many different areas; for allowing my children to be brought up in a home that was so unsettled; for not taking the time to do a simple thing like pray and wait on the Lord!

I was sincerely angry with myself for years. Here I thought I was so smart and yet, how easily did I get duped? It didn't matter that evidence of God's forgiveness, His grace and His mercy were evident in my life, or that He was in fact still blessing me and my family. He was still answering prayers and guiding me through life, but because of my husband's still unsaved state, I couldn't see my blessings, so I just didn't feel forgivable or **forgiven**. All I felt was constant anger. It happened every time my husband and I argued over why I felt it was inappropriate to celebrate Halloween, the kind of TV shows that were appropriate for the family, the music the kids listened to, the places they were allowed to go, the arguments about paying tithes, the importance of a Christian education, or the arguments we had about the importance of church attendance (this sort of argument use to happen whenever the kids wanted to stay home on Sunday with him).

The weight of it all became increasingly unbearable. I wasn't living a victorious life, no matter how big my smile on Sunday morning, or how many poems I wrote, encouragement I gave, or Sunday school classes I taught, I was not joyful and it was tearing me up on the inside and was slowly but surely starting to be evident on the outside.

I felt myself slipping into depression. To be honest, I was seriously depressed for a number of years. I gained a lot of weight and my appearance went down the toilet. I didn't care what I looked like. I was a sight to see! I even went to the doctor for an official diagnosis. I was prescribed an anti-depressant and that prescription opened my eyes. I started to question my faith. Why was I, a child of the King, about to rely on pills to be "happy"?[1] It was pure revelation that made me realize that my problem was me and my anger with myself. But how was I going to forgive me for putting the kids and me in what I felt was an impossible situation? Here was an instance where I had to let go and let God literally. I had to step out on faith and let go of that sin that truly had me bound. It took some time, but step by step I learned to

> "But the LORD still waits for you to come to him so he can show you his love and compassion. For the LORD is a faithful God. Blessed are those who wait for him to help them."
> - Isaiah 30:18 (NLT)

---

[1] This is not to say that Christians can't and don't suffer from depression and that there aren't times when medication and/or therapy are needed to overcome that thing that has you bound. It does not have to mean that you lack faith. Depression can be a mentally crippling condition that can leave you physically ill, and will take time to overcome. But with God and prayer it is a battle that can be won.

21

forgive myself. I'm learning to trust in Jesus, his promises and the simple power of His name.

I thank God for using authors like Charles Stanley (*The Gift of Forgiveness, 1987*) to help me to see what was right in front of me all along. I tell you I could literally feel the weight being lifted from my shoulders when I started to forgive myself.

As you have just read, I experienced some classic symptoms of an unforgiving spirit towards oneself. I punished myself over and over again. Each time I recalled my sin, I allowed the enemy to use it to keep me down. I also developed a sense of unworthiness, which was the very reason I didn't seek God's forgiveness initially. And even after I did go to him for forgiveness, I still felt the need to continue on my own course of punishment. Because I kept recalling my sinful decision, I kept asking, why would God be so forgiving? Again, the enemy was at work and I just kept spiraling downward.

I deprived myself of all things enjoyable. As I worked to give myself a sufficient punishment, my feelings of unworthiness grew and so did my believing that I was not forgiven or even my right to ask for God's forgiveness. This state of mind caused me to have a terrible prayer life and I lost connection with the Father because I didn't believe in the total healing power of His forgiveness. I didn't exercise an ounce of faith in His forgiveness being unconditional, total and complete. Therefore, the enemy was able to use me against myself and I lost precious time and fellowship with God. It wasn't that God ever left me or didn't forgive me, it was the other way around. Because of unbelief and not understanding who God is and how He works, I suffered years of self-inflicted pain. The punishments I heaped on myself had nothing to do with the consequences of my action, because God didn't need any help from me!

The importance of forgiveness cannot be overstated.

1. When you have sinned, no matter what it is, go to the Father for forgiveness and know that you have been forgiven.

2. When necessary forgive the offender, in this instance, you must forgive your spouse for deceiving you (if that is the case). In some instances they may have deceived themselves. Whether intentional or not, they may have thought they were a Christian because of bad teaching or Satan's deception. Whatever the circumstance, you have to forgive them (Matthew 6:14-15).

3. Lastly forgive yourself and allow the Lord to heal you from the inside out.

As I come to the end of this chapter, I would love to tell you that miraculously I have never returned to that way of thinking, but this walk is real, and that would not be true. So I admit, there are times when I slip back into the past because of some recent altercation, and I start to feel that old hurt again about the choice I made. Also true is the fact that when I do find myself slipping back into that negative way of thinking, I have noticed that it is when I have started to lose focus on Jesus. It is when my prayer life and my reading of the Word are not consistent. It is during those times that mess can creep in. In other words, the enemy never sleeps, therefore, there is no place for complacency ever, and your prayer life and the reading of God's Word is always, always, ALWAYS important.

> [20]*Moreover the law entered, that the offence might abound. But where sin abounded, grace did much more abound:*
>
> *Romans 5:20*

always, always, ALWAYS important. I thank God for His grace and mercy, because without it, I truly don't know where I would be.

Allowing God's love to heal your heart and mind is what is going to enable you to stand strong through the next step of this healing process, which is the daily living with the consequences of your disobedience. Living with the fallout is what I call being "in the valley," and there are some important tools that are needed in order to live in the valley victoriously. Just because you are in the valley does not mean that you have to live a defeated or depressed life, but you will need the whole armor of God to survive.

STEP TWO: *Forgiveness frees you from sin and shame, so seek God's forgiveness, and let go of your hurt and shame so that you can forgive yourself.*

Reflection: Have you noticed a lagging fellowship with God in your life since you became involved with an unsaved partner? If so, is it because you have been ashamed to fellowship with Him based on your marital situation?

Do you feel yourself slipping or have you slipped into a mental and/or physical state of depression because of guilt or anger with yourself?

Were there opportunities and blessings in the past that you now realize were missed due to self-punishment and lack of forgiveness?

Are you willing to seek God, confess your sin and allow him to give you the power to forgive your spouse and yourself?

Discussion: The most important thing for you is to realize is God's readiness and willingness to forgive you. You cannot expect your Christian walk to get any better without His forgiveness. It is what ultimately sets you free and allows you to begin the healing process.

After reflecting on this chapter, take some prayer time to reconnect with God, ask for His forgiveness, go spend some time in His word and allow Him to give you the power to forgive yourself.

Chapter III

In the Valley

*A*s I mentioned in the previous chapter, God's forgiveness of our sin does not release us from the consequences of our actions. I am going to begin this chapter with a couple of verses that are applicable to this discussion:

Hebrews 12:6 (NKJV)
"For whom the Lord loves He chastens, and scourges every son whom he receives."

Hebrews 12:11
"Now no chastening for the present seemeth to be joyous, but grievous: nevertheless afterward it yieldeth the peaceable fruit of righteousness unto them which are exercised thereby."

What is God telling us? What truth do we need to gain from these passages?

Expect His Hand of Correction

I believe that He wants His children to know that no sin will go unpunished, as He molds us and shapes us into the children He knows we can be. There are some lessons for us to learn through our disobedience, and the hand of correction is ever there to help us grow! Of course, there are some lessons that we learn that have nothing to do with our committing sins. There are just some things that happen in life, like sicknesses, death of a loved one, job loss, etc. Sometimes bad things just happen. In fact, the Bible tells us that we are troubled on every hand, but it is important that we realize that everything bad that happens is not a direct result of disobedience.

But marrying an unsaved person is one of those blatant acts of disobedience where the hand of correction should be expected, and in most cases, I would think that the hand of correction is really painful!

My Chastisement

My act of disobedience was by omission. I did not intentionally or actively set out to betray God, but by not doing my homework and losing focus, the results were still the same. I chose to close my eyes to all the obvious signs. As a very dear friend said, "Bottom line it was your responsibility to make sure his walk was real!" Because I failed to stand on God's promises, I sowed the wind and reaped the whirlwind!

It took less than four months for me to realize the honeymoon was over! My new husband stopped going to church immediately and started hanging out all hours of the night. My head was reeling. Literally, my world began to fall apart. Over the next few months, I realized that he was indeed serious about no longer attending church. I asked him why he stopped. I reminded him of our conversations where we both said that we wanted a family that went to church together. His answer was that he had made a mistake; he thought he wanted all that, but he just wasn't ready to make that kind of decision. Make that kind of decision?! Didn't he realize that one of the reasons I married him was because of his profession of salvation, and that we would be a family that worshipped and prayed together?!

Sure he did. That is why he was so good at attending church prior to the marriage. It's why he made sure we attended the church he had grown up in, where everybody, including the pastor, knew his name. I mean his entire family was well-known in the congregation. But it was all a lie. I know why I wanted to be married, but his exact reason I couldn't tell you because he obviously still wanted to live the single life. And it would be two long years of crying, yelling, screaming, infidelity and then a year's separation before he stopped hanging out in the streets and started acting like a husband. My immediate sentence was a term of three years. After that came probation and the time for that has yet to be determined.

Sadly, it was not until that year of separation that I finally prayed! I spent so much time in the Word and in prayer, it was almost fanatical. I had nowhere else to turn. Initially, I didn't pray because of the guilt I felt—guilt that moved in after it all hit the fan and sat on my shoulders continuously. It weighed down on me heavily and the immense shame kept me from even seeking forgiveness, let alone seeking God's counsel. I honestly felt that I had no right to run to God for help, it took me a couple of years to see the error of my thinking and that's when I decided to go to the Source. Here I was newly married, separated and to top it all off, I was pregnant! The consequences of marrying out of God's will made themselves evident in the most painful of ways, and I just knew I was about to be divorced. What's more, I wanted one! Anything to wake up from the nightmare.

But God!

During my times of prayer, reading and reflection, I honestly wanted a way out, but more than that, I found that the more I prayed, what I wanted most was to please God, and slowly my prayer focus changed from self to wanting what His will was for my life and for my marriage. The more I prayed in this manner, I felt no signs that God

> [3]We can rejoice, too, when we run into problems and trials, for we know that they are good for us–they help us learn to endure. [4]And endurance develops strength of character in us, and character strengthens our confident expectation of salvation. [5]And this expectation will not disappoint us. For we know how dearly God loves us, because he has given us the Holy Spirit to fill our hearts with his love. [6]When we were utterly helpless, Christ came at just the right time and died for us sinners.
> -Romans 5:3-6 (NLT)

was going to be granting me the out that I so diligently sought. He spoke loud and clear—I was going to work on my marriage. The die had been cast, and it was now time to do what I should have done in the beginning, lean on and trust in Him.

While I was separated, if you were not a believer, I did not discuss my situation with you. And there were only a few saints that knew the full details. From the moment my husband and I separated, I was convicted of keeping all non-believers out of my business. That was hard, as my life at the time consisted of a lot of close unsaved acquaintances. Some acquaintances, because of my silence, stopped speaking to me for a while—in fact, one older woman, with whom I really thought we were on the way to becoming good friends, has never spoken to me again.

Initially, it hurt and I did miss her, but none of that mattered to me. The rejection I felt from her wasn't as strong as my resolve to heed the voice that told me to avoid conversation with an unbeliever concerning my marriage. I was convicted and convinced that secular advice was to be avoided like the plague. I am truly thankful that I heeded that voice.

Face God's Punishment

When you are going through a trial, you have to be careful that you are not giving ground to Satan. Discussing biblical things with people of unbelief gets you advice that is not biblical and/or only fuels *your* flesh and *your* will. It amazed me that even through my heartache; my desire was still to please God. To me that was a positive sign that God was not through with me yet.

People who don't believe (and even some who do) will tell you; "Leave that man alone. Get a divorce. If my husband cheated on me, I'd be walking. Besides, he lied to you in the first place about being saved. God understands these things child, dump him." And the bad advice goes on and on. None of that advice is scriptural and you don't need to hear it. You need to concentrate on what "sayeth the Lord." Period.

> [21] *There are many devices in a man's heart; nevertheless the counsel of the LORD, that shall stand.*
> Proverbs 19:21 (KJV)

"For better or worse" means just that. And until and when we turn our eyes on Jesus, there will be no relief from the "worse." Until we learn to wait and not go forward on our strength, the trials and tribulations that are inevitable will always seem bigger than life, the mountains higher, and the valleys wider and lower. Isaiah 40:31 is God's promise to those who wait and trust in Him. It is His promise to give us the strength, and the power to make it through the "worst" of times.

"But those that wait on the Lord shall renew their strength; they shall mount up with wings like eagles, they shall run and not be weary, they shall walk and not faint." (NKJV)

During the separation, God worked on me and He also worked on my husband, and although He has yet to bring him to salvation. He helped him to grow up. My husband realized that he wanted to live in the same house as his newly born son. He wanted to be an active participant in the raising of his children. Slowly, but surely after we decided to make a go of our marriage, my husband stopped staying out late at night and he stopped going out so often. His behavior became more of a husband and a devoted father. To sum it all up, he stopped acting like a jerk! And I knew it had to be God. Who else can change a man's heart and his behavior? And who besides God can change an unsaved man's behavior to that of a responsible husband and father in a short period of time?

I am not saying that our lives have been a fairytale since we reconciled, because they have not. Far from it. Through the years we have considered divorce and separation on numerous occasions. But God has allowed me to have some moments of peace through the years, but those moments are just that— moments. Our spirits are at war and the war will never cease as long as he serves darkness and I serve light. I would not have you ignorant sisters, the struggle is constant and never ending. There is always a new battle between us and those battles are fierce! I am ever reminded that my husband does not know Jesus and that is a hard thing to live with, but like I said, some consequences can be for an indefinite amount of time.

Consequences: I cannot go to my husband and discuss things that were said in the sermon. I can't go to him with prayer requests or any sort of guidance concerning scripture or decisions that have to be made for the family. We can't even talk about things that are going on in the world that have biblical application, because we don't believe the same thing. That is a hard pill to swallow on a daily basis. I ache inside when I have to attend events at the church by myself or just the kids and me. I ache when there are couple retreats that I cannot participate in. And the consequences continue: I miss a lot of church outings because my husband doesn't know Christ, and being around "church people" makes him uncomfortable. My husband's negative attitude about church and its people is something that the children hear and see. Yet with all the negative that I get from him, I know that doesn't mean that the Lord isn't working on his heart. At the same time, I also know his salvation isn't promised. The reality of it all is that there is a war going on in my household every day and at times I get so tired that I just want to throw up my hands and say, "Enough already! I give up!"

Again I say: but God! It is my earnest prayer to stand while I am in this valley. Standing isn't and won't always be easy, but I know that if I keep the faith and believe in the words that the Lord gave us to live by, I will be able to withstand against the fiery darts that the enemy is going to send. In *2 Corinthians 4:8-9 (NKJV), it states: "We are hard-pressed on every side, yet not crushed; we are perplexed, but not in despair; persecuted, but not forsaken; struck down, but not destroyed.* These verses are words of victory! They tell God's children that no matter the circumstances, we can stand strong because God is all the strength that we need. Yes, we go through many kinds of heartaches and sorrows, but they are not, they do not, and should not define who we are in Christ. All this stuff on earth is temporary and is nothing compared to the eternal rewards waiting for those who endure.

Standing Firm While In the Valley

We have talked about the various consequences that I have endured, but let me tell you how I endure them. It is not because I am strong in and of myself. It is because I found out about the armor that God has laid out for His children.

Ephesians 6:14-18 (NKJV)

First, you have to have your "loins girt about with truth." This is the belt in the suit of armor, which also serves to support the remaining armor. It is important to have the belt of Truth, which is Jesus. You have to know in your heart that Jesus is the Truth and the only way to the Father. To know Jesus is to know truth and God is truth. Your very foundation is based in Jesus and your belief in Him and in God who sent him.

Next, you need the "breastplate of righteousness," which protects the heart and other vital organs. What is righteousness? It is simply doing things the right way and the right way is the way of God. This you must know in your heart, as it is vital, like the heart is to your survival.

Also, you need your "feet shod with the preparation of the gospel of peace." Always be prepared to proclaim the gospel; telling people of Jesus and His love that is available to all. Even in the times of trials, let the love of Jesus be seen in you. No matter the current circumstance of your life, you must be ready to show God's love so that you are able to share it with those in need. Next, you need the "shield of faith." Simply, put all your faith in God. Give him your total and absolute trust. With the shield, you will be able to withstand the continual assaults of the wicked,

35

which are sure to bombard you, especially in a home that's divided.

In addition, you will need the "helmet of salvation." The helmet gives you the assurance of your salvation. Knowing that you know you are saved protects the mind. And this is important, for the battle that we fight against the enemy is won and/or lost in our minds. *"For we wrestle not against flesh and blood, but with principalities and wickedness in high places, that cannot be seen with the human eye."* Remember that discouragement and doubt are tools of the enemy. That is why the helmet is so necessary—it protects the mind!

Then you will need the "sword of the Spirit, which is the word of God." My pastor says that the Word will either draw you or make you run. Allow the Holy Spirit in your life on a daily basis through the reading of God's Word. Allow it to draw you even closer to the one who can do anything but fail.

Lastly, in order to hold this armor together successfully, you have to pray. Stay on your knees! Don't play down how you really feel. You can be brutally honest with God. Pray without ceasing! It is through prayer that you maintain fellowship with the Father. And when you pray, don't be afraid to let the Lord know your needs. Be ever watchful, so that you don't give ground to the enemy.

For the Woman Married to an Unsaved Man
We have now acknowledged our consequences and know what it takes to live with them victoriously. But, and I speak only to

women now, there is one more thing that I believe can assist you in being truly victorious. Submission. Being submissive to your husband is only a small part of the submission process. First, you must be submissive to God and His will for you in the marriage.

One of the older women in my church gave me a book, *Liberated Through Submission*, 1990, by P. B. Wilson. It took me over an entire year to read that book. I put the book on the shelf. Looked at it occasionally as I walked past, but that's all I did was look. The last thing I wanted to do was to read a book that I *assumed* was going to tell me about cow-towing to my jerk of a husband. And with his not being saved, I totally balked at the very notion (But you know, both my assumption and my attitude were wrong).

One day, after about a year or so, the Lord led me to read that book, and it turned out to be one of the best blessings in my life. The way Mrs. Wilson laid out submission opened my eyes to a whole new way of thinking and it helped me to look at submission in a brand new and positive light. She started by laying out three principles, 1) Submission is for everyone, 2) Submission plus faith equals power, and 3) Submission plus power equals liberation. She goes on to define and gets into what it really means to submit and in her words, there really was liberation.

For the purpose of the healing process that I am writing about, my focus is on submission on the part of the wife to the husband, specifically, the saved wife to the unsaved husband.

I Peter 3:1-2 (NKJV)
Wives, likewise, be submissive to your own
husbands, that even if some do not obey the word,
they, without a word, may be won by the conduct of
their wives, when they observe your chaste conduct
accompanied by fear.

The Lord commands us to treat our "unsaved" husbands with all due respect *as unto Him.* In this we may win our husbands to Christ by our conduct. If our husbands see us expressing Godly behavior and walking it like we talk it, we set the stage for the possibility of our husbands' coming to Christ. Our spouses' coming to a saving knowledge should always be our heartfelt desire and prayer, but we should also be cognizant of the fact that it is not promised that our unsaved spouses will come to know Christ. It's not written anywhere in the Word that God will save your spouse. This is why it is so very important not to become unequally yoked in the first place. Read the passage again. It says, "that they may be won…." It does not say, "they will" be won. In 1 Corinthians 7:16, the Bible puts a question to you: *"How do you know, O wife, whether you will save your husband?"* If your unsaved spouses wishes to remain, then you are to allow it. Basically, work on your marriage!

Although there are no guarantees of salvation for that unsaved spouse, it is imperative that you do your part and be the type of witness who can at least set the stage where acceptance is a possibility. In the next chapter, we will be discussing the tongue, which is important because that little member can cause a lot of friction, resulting in the near impossibility for leading your spouse to Christ.

I wrote the poems at the end of this chapter when I was at great odds, yet again, with my husband. I was feeling really depressed and hating myself for allowing myself to be so thoroughly duped. I was feeling trapped and I wanted out! I just wanted some peace. The constant battles between my husband and me were getting old and I wanted the Lord to release me. Of course, it had to be biblical, which only increased my dilemma, because biblically, there was no way out that I could see.

As usual, God was not listening to that kind of request. As I began to reflect, I could hear Him comforting me by bringing to remembrance the many valleys He had already brought me through since I became unequally yoked. I could hear Him so clearly telling me that I wasn't alone. In the subconscious I knew this, but in the here and now, I wasn't feeling it.

The Lord reminded me of the many blessings in my life—good health, food and shelter, a well-paying job, saved friends, a church home that doesn't water down the gospel, good children, just to name a few. But before I could see any of that, I had to learn about the sufficiency of God's grace. I had to learn to be like Paul, content in whatever state I find myself (Philippians 4:11). I can truly say that I have experienced this kind of contentment for periods of time in my life, but my goal is to feel this type of contentment constantly, whether the tides are high or low. (2 Corinthians 12:9-10)

Having said all that, I wrote "In the Valley," and "A Prayer for Peace" when I felt like I was sinking fast. Maybe you can relate to some of the emotions I experienced.

Brothers and sisters, our goal is to be angry and sin not, to cry and yet be able to smile in spite of, to experience that joy unspeakable when the world around you seems ready to explode! Each of us needs to realize that even in our valleys we can have victory and an inner peace and a joy that is inexplicable.

And also know this (not by way of justification), whether you are married to an unsaved spouse or not, there are going to be some visits to the valley. "In the Valley" is applicable as you go through whatever trial you're experiencing. The poem simply reminds us that no matter what we go through, our goal is to...stand. God has not promised any of his children a life without obstacles, but He has promised never to leave nor forsake us. God has given each of us the tools and the strength needed to handle adversity in a virtuous manner.

[13] *But remember that the temptations that come into your life are no different from what others experience. And God is faithful. He will keep the temptation from becoming so strong that you can't stand up against it. When you are tempted, he will show you a way out so that you will not give in to it.*
1 Corinthians 10:13

Step Three: *Every choice comes with consequences, learn to stand firm while facing those consequences. Allow God to chastise and to refine you for His purpose.*

Reflections: Have there been certain trials, or are you going through something right now that you recognize as a consequence and relate to being God's hand of correction in your life?

What are some long-term consequences that you have had to face since you married your unsaved spouse?

What do you do or what have you found are successful means to endure while living "In the Valley?"

What are other ways in which you can be a Godly witness to your spouse and family?

Discussion: Facing God's chastisement is hard, but always keep in mind that God loves those who he chastens. Whatever consequences you face in life, they are not there to trouble you, but to ultimately refine you. That is why it is important to know that you will face consequences for disobedience, but doubly important to learn from those consequences and rightly inform those in danger of making the same mistake.

It might be cliché, but take the time to reverence God for chastening you. And, begin to arm yourself spiritually so that you can endure the short and long-term consequences of being unequally yoked.

41

In the Valley

The storms of life rage all around me;
I barely know up from down.
Yet, I know in my heart that Jesus has the
power to turn things around.

The winds of life blow hard against me, at
times the force knocks me to my knees.
That's when the Lord speaks to my heart and
says, "My grace is sufficient for thee."

Because it's sufficient, I somehow rise and
manage to stand tall.
I take a deep breath, tighten my armor
and heed to His call.

It is my prayer that Jesus hearkens to my voice
and hears my earnest plea.
Although the going is rough, whilst I'm in
this valley, I yearn for Victory.

A Prayer for Peace

Help me Lord, I don't know how
Much longer I can hold on.
My countenance is low, and I feel
Battered and torn.

Physically my body is tired and my mind
Feels like it's about to explode!
With thoughts of despair that leave me
Shaking with fear; they leave me feeling cold.

This burden grows heavier with each passing day;
Only you know how I even manage to pray.
I'm relying on your promise that you would never
Leave me alone; that you're with me, come what may.

I'm crying out to you, Jesus; for only through prayer
Can I find a measure of relief.
Please help me to carry some of this load
For your child needs some moments of peace.

Undeserving, yes, as I chose not to obey your
Word, this torment is only just
But nonetheless, it's mercy I seek; and it's in your
Grace that I'm putting all my trust.

Chapter IV

Taming the Untamable

James 3:5-6

*Even so the tongue is a little member and boasts
great things. See how great a forest a little fire
kindles! And the tongue is a fire, a world of
iniquity. The tongue is so set among our members
that it defiles the whole body, and sets on fire the
course of nature; and it is set on fire by hell.*

I believe commenting on the tongue is important because the
tongue has the power to build up and to tear down. And
while we are in the valley, we are learning to deal with choices we
have made, so it is very easy to unconsciously try to transmit some
of that hurt and frustration we may be feeling to someone else.
This whole book is about healing and coming to grips with an

unwise choice. It is about learning to live with the consequences that come with bad decisions. Therefore, it is important to recognize where we are in our healing process, as it can help us to be aware of the things we are thinking and feeling in hopes that they don't end up being verbalized in the wrong way.

Having said that, Ladies, having the last word is not all it's cracked up to be. And as women, most, if not all of us love to have the last word, sometimes to our very detriment. We must learn to control our tongues!

The Power of the Tongue

James tells us that that little member can start a raging fire…from hell. In other words, we need to think before we speak because the enemy is ever present seeking to devour, to steal our joy, to kill in deed, if possible and to destroy our walk. Satan knows that the smallest comment taken or said out of context can start the fires raging in our homes. This holds true in life as a whole. We will be held accountable for *every* idle word that we say. Knowing this, it is important that we monitor our mouths and the words that proceed.

One great truth for us is to always be mindful that our spouses do not know Jesus. Accordingly, their thoughts, their very actions don't come under the same authority. What I am saying is that we can count on them to do and say things that are just plain contrary. How we handle what is done and/or said is what makes the difference. How we respond verbally can either sooth or inflame.

Being married to an unsaved spouse puts you constantly in the hot box. Whether you feel it fair or unfair, right or wrong, your partner, whether they say it or not, is watching you with eagle eyes and listening with the same sharp ears.

[14]In everything you do, stay away from complaining and arguing, [15]so that no one can speak a word of blame against you. You are to live clean, innocent lives as children of God in a dark world full of crooked and perverse people. Let your lives shine brightly before them.
Philippians 2:14-15 (NLT)

Everything you do and say is being taken to heart. How you respond to life's stresses, other people, at home, on your job, etc., they are paying attention. They are looking for every reason to tell you why being saved isn't necessary or such a big deal. Your tongue could be a hindrance, if you are not mindful of the way you speak to or the tones you use with your spouse. Not to mention the things you let fly out of your mouth in the midst of arguments. Bringing up the past is NOT productive in a disagreement, nor is talking down to or at your spouse.

Learning to temper your words with salt will take conscious effort on your part—action. Yes, there are times when it seems like your spouse is just lying in wait for you to pick an argument, but remember, the enemy stays on the prowl for the destruction of the home. You have to remind yourself that often it isn't your spouse but rather the enemy working through them to get at you. The enemy wants you to continue the vicious cycle of non-productiveness in your marriage, which makes him happy, as it eats at a foundation that the Lord holds in the highest esteem, the family. Keeping this thought forefront can help us to remain vigilant of what we are thinking, so that if necessary, we'd choose to bite our tongues before making a comment that could set you back months and or even years in your relationship.

Tempering Your Words with Salt

Looking through the book of Proverbs, I found excellent advice when it comes to the mouth and our tongues! I have included a few that can be committed to memory.

Proverbs 21:23
"Whoever guards his mouth and tongue keeps his soul from troubles."

I find this verse pretty self-explanatory, but for clarification so there's no misunderstanding, we would do a lot less apologizing, and deal with a lot less fallout from arguments, if we'd only learn what to say and how to say it. If we did just a bit more thinking before we spoke, a lot of the battles we've lost with the enemy would be victories. We wouldn't be avoiding people and regretting words that can come so callously out of our mouths. Because once the words have left our lips, there is no taking them back. The tone we use will be heard possibly for days, weeks or even years by the recipient.

Proverbs 18:6
"A fool's lips enter into contention [controversy]."

Short, sweet and to the point, but a little elaborating can't hurt. Sometimes we run our mouths constantly about nothing instead of being examples of what we want our spouses to believe in. Speaking without a thought or care is only going to cause additional tension in your marriage. Your spouse is more interested in what you do and say outside of church than your verbal professions of faith and the love of God. Words spoken in an unwise manner can stir up quite a mess in the home, so again I say, think before you speak!

Proverbs 15:1
"A soft answer turns away wrath, but a harsh word
stirs up anger."

Often is not what you say but how you say it. This includes the volume that is used. Be honest, women, we are prone to drama at times, which in turn causes us to speak in tones much louder or harsher than necessary. And we often do it in the wrong place and at the wrong time. If you don't want your spouse speaking to you in a raised voice or a harsh tone, what makes you think they want to be spoken to in the same fashion? Or in front of an audience? Being right isn't important all the time, and being right doesn't mean being the one who speaks the loudest or nastiest! Along with good listening skills, some of us could use some lessons on how to talk to people. And not just our spouses, people in general. Over the years, I have learned that my delivery makes all the difference in whether I get a positive or negative response. Pick your battles wisely and consider your words at all times, because the wrong words said in the heat of the moment can have long-lasting repercussions.

Proverbs 17:28
"Even a fool is counted wise when he holds his peace; when he shuts his lips, he is considered perceptive."

Now those words are on the money. Holding your tongue may cause some hurt to your ego and/or pride, but can save you a boatload of trouble and apologies.

Proverbs 15:4
"A wholesome tongue is a tree of life, but perverseness in it breaks the spirit."

You have heard it said, "If you don't have anything nice to say, say nothing at all." In this verse, I believe the Lord is reminding us of this. Words can and do hurt and certain things said in a particular manner can wound a person's spirit—sometimes causing damage that can take years to overcome. A wholesome tongue isn't going to spew out negativity. It considers its words carefully, because it knows that a response that doesn't come from a spirit of edification can do a lot more harm than good. I know that it is human nature to respond to negative comments in like manner, but for the saint, it should not be so. We are called to a higher purpose. For which cause, we are to be more vigilant, for we desire or should desire to be like Christ in all things.

My pastor once said, "A need of a man is praise and honor." Use your tongue to encourage and lift your spouse up for what they do. Sometimes we miss the good things because we are so focused on the bad.

These are just a few of the verses that I believe would be beneficial for recall when you are tempted to say something that would be better left unsaid. True, your thoughts are your own, but a little work on knowing how, when to verbalize and when not to verbalize, couldn't hurt.

Step Four: *Learn to temper your tongue; do not give your spouse excuse to fine fault in your Christian walk by finding fault in your speech.*

Reflections: In what ways have found the tongue to be a powerful weapon in distancing your spouse from you and God?

Are there spiteful things you have said to your spouse in the past that you could ask forgiveness for?

Knowing the enemy likes to cause discord in your relationship, what are ways in which you can prevent discussions from getting too heated?

What are some ways in which you can encourage your spouse on a daily basis?

Discussions: Again, remember that your spouse does not know God, and therefore is not under the same authority as you, so taming you tongue is going to be a battle. Reflect on these Proverbs at all times when dealing with your spouse.

Take time and think of your spouse's good qualities, then somewhere along the way compliment and encourage those qualities. After all, you married them for some of those good qualities, right?

Chapter 17
He's Still Calling Your Name

***N**ews flash!* Just because you went ahead and married a partner that God did not give his okay to, does not mean that He does not love you and that He cannot and will not use you for His glory. As I mentioned previously, you will have some consequences to deal with, but that does not mean that God isn't still calling your name. It does not mean that you aren't going to do great things for the Lord, such as become a missionary, cut a CD, write a book, be a teacher, or even become a great evangelist. In other words, disobedience is not a license to give up. We all fall down at one time or another.

> *[16a]For a just man falleth seven times, and riseth up again...*
> *Proverbs 24:16a (KJV)*

Whether or not you stay down is the issue.

It is human nature to wallow in self-pity, but it is not what God wants us to do, nor is it very productive. Especially when you are

53

going through a storm, self-pity can make a mild thunderstorm seem like a hurricane. Pity parties are just another tool of the enemy to have us focus on our failures, when we should be finding out how to make lemonade out of our lemons!

Submit to God and Stand on His Promises

Are you asking how? First of all, it will take some action on your part. You are going to have to put forth some physical effort. Sitting on your hands waiting for a magic wand of change is not going to get you the victory you want or need to help you through the battlefield. A change in attitude is something that can help you see things in a brighter light. A positive attitude can make your whole outlook change from hopeless to hopeful. If you start standing on the promises of God, your countenance cannot help but change. There is always hope to be found in God's Word, as in I Corinthians 7:12-14,16 (NKJV):

> *But to the rest I, not the Lord, say: If any brother has a wife who does not believe, and she is willing to live with him, let him not divorce her. [13]And a woman who has a husband who does not believe, if he is willing to live with her, let her not divorce him. For the unbelieving husband is sanctified by the wife, and the unbelieving wife is sanctified by the husband; otherwise your children would be unclean, but now they are holy.*

*For how do you know, O wife, whether you will
save your husband? Or how do you know, O
husband, whether you will save your wife?*

The Word is telling us in these verses that there is hope and reminds us that our attitudes and behavior play a part in the possibility of our spouses' coming to salvation. This is the action part I spoke of earlier. You have to decide to be obedient to God's Word, which means consciously working on your behavior, for women it means submitting to your spouse, for men it means loving your spouse. Their being unsaved does not give you license to run the ship. This was hard for me to accept. I had no confidence in any of my husband's decisions. I always doubted his doing what was best for the family as a whole. But once I made a decision to change my focus from submitting to my husband, per se, to submitting to God's will, it slowly but surely became easier to allow my husband to lead (continues to be work in progress).

When you change your focus to submitting to God, He can make it so your spouse does the right thing more often than not. Your submission to God can have your unsaved partner tithing/and or giving large amounts to the church when they would really rather not. As previously mentioned, *Liberated Through Submission* by P. B. Wilson, was instrumental in helping me to change my attitude regarding submission as a whole, but more pointedly towards submitting to my husband.

Praise God in Your Circumstance

Next, we have to learn to praise God anyhow! That means no matter what we are going through, we have to praise God continually. In Hebrews 13:15, the Bible tells us to "continually offer the sacrifice of praise to God, that is the fruit of our lips, giving thanks to His name." If we are busy praising God, we won't have time for complaining, wallowing in guilt, shame, doubt, etc. We can do this through prayer, the Word, reading Christian/inspirational books, listening to gospel/Christian music, hymns and/or psalms. Learning to praise God when you don't want to do anything but cry and mope takes work! Because when we feel bad, we don't feel like praising. We would rather go with that helpless "poor me" attitude, or pull out the old R&B tunes, and from there we can almost assuredly spiral down into an abyss of "woe is me!"

I love music, so it became imperative that I change the words that were coming into my hearing. When I feel like I am about to go down for the count, I blast my gospel music! I start out with fast-paced selections, which get me ready for the slower selections, which get me ready for some serious praising! I find gospel music to be soothing and cleansing and over the years, through many trials, gospel music has become my first choice in music. It feeds my wounded spirit and just puts me in a mood to praise and thank God. It helps me to remember whose child I am and that with God all things are possible! Gospel music helps me to remember to count my blessings. I am not suggesting that my method is "the way." I am just sharing some of the things I do to keep the demons at bay.

Purify Your Body and Mind

Secular forms of entertainment will not help you tap into Jesus and neither will other ungodly avenues of escape. When you are

> [23] Above all else, guard your heart, for it is the wellspring of life. [24] Put away perversity from your mouth; keep corrupt talk far from your lips. [25] Let your eyes look straight ahead, fix your gaze directly before you. [26] Make level paths for your feet and take only ways that are firm.
> - Proverbs 4:23-26 (NIV)

up close and personal with tough times, and the enemy is after you in full force, you can only fight successfully when you keep your mind on the things of God.

Remember, you cannot defeat the enemy by human means. You must keep your mind on spiritual things. So I say crank up the gospel!

Make no mistake about it. Satan desires to sift us like wheat! That is why studying God's Word is so essential in the life of the believer. It can't be said enough, read your Word daily! The Word is what helps to keep you on track, along with its partner, prayer.

Learn Your Gifts

Concentrate on them and pray for guidance. Find out what the Lord wants you to do with your gift(s). Believe me, He has a plan. He is just waiting patiently to see if you will take the time to seek Him out and find out the plan. Knowing the talents that God has given to you is worth the time it takes to find out what they are. As I said, I love music. Does it mean I can sing? No, so I owe it to myself and my close friends to find out my true calling. You don't want to spend a lot of time and effort on something that may interest you, but it is evident that it is not your gift or where the Lord would have you concentrate most of your energy. Ask your pastor or a member of his staff to help you with this. I am sure that they can offer you assistance as you seek God's will for your life. I know there are surveys out there with questions that you answer that can help to point you in the right direction. I have even seen a spiritual gift questionnaire on the internet!

You are God's Child

It is all about focus or re-focusing your mind to the One who is able to do exceedingly, abundantly above all that you ask. The more you focus on God and His will for your life, the easier your trials will be to bear. No, the trials won't cease, but you will be able to stand through them. The power that you need to stand strong is in the very name of Jesus! Call on Him and give Him an opportunity to help you live the kind of victorious life you were meant to live. By victorious, I mean the ability to stand through times of adversity.

"I am the vine, ye are the branches: He that abideth in me, and I in him, the same bringeth forth much fruit: for without me ye can do nothing."
John 15: 5

John 15:5 tells us that apart from God we can do nothing. It does not say, we can do a little, or some, it says nothing! We have to connect to the vine, which is Christ, and seek His will daily and we will be able to withstand the trickery of Satan. The Lord can and will use you to advance His kingdom if you give Him a chance. Your marrying an unsaved spouse is not enough to separate you from Christ. You need the confidence of Paul:

> "For I am persuaded neither death, nor life, nor angels, nor principalities, nor powers, nor things present, nor things to come, nor height, nor depth, nor any other creature (this includes you), shall be able to separate us from the love of God, which is in Christ." – Romans 8:38

After all that, what could we mere mortals do to separate us from our Heavenly Father? Nothing! Hallelujah!!

Close your eyes. Relax in a quiet place and you will hear Him calling your name. God doesn't leave us, we leave Him. He doesn't stop calling, we stop listening. And the reasons we leave or stop listening are guilt, a lack of faith and unbelief. But we need to remember that we are not the first children to be disobedient and we won't be the last.

The Bible is full of people who stepped out of God's will, yet the Lord used them for great things. The Old Testament is full of men of great faith who were overcome with human failings at least once. David is a prime example of a man who loved God but allowed his lust for another man's wife to cause him to commit sin on top of sin. His consequences were severe, but God still used him, and David knew the Lord was with him until the day he died. David knew that he was the sinner and he accepted his consequences, for he knew that he and only he had sinned against God. He humbled himself and went to God for forgiveness. He admitted his sins, and God still used David in a mighty way. He did not remove his consequences, but what is more important is that he did not remove his love and protection. David knew God loved him even after all that he had done. That is why David praised God continually.

Moses suffered from a lack of confidence in himself, which in turn made him question God, and he had a temper, and his temper on occasion caused him to strike out with his own brand of reprimand, yet the Lord constantly used him. But you know the story, he struck out one time too many and it caused him not enter into the promised land. God's mercy allowed him to see it but he was not able to enter in. I am sure this grieved God more than Moses, but as a Father, He had to do what He did, because you cannot sin against God without some sort of reprimand. The reprimand that Moses received and that we receive are direct results of decisions that we make. We decide to go against God, whether consciously or not, we choose disobedience, and disobedience comes with a price. And yet, after or all during the consequence, the Lord is still able to use His "hard-headed" children in monumental ways.

In the New Testament, when Christ was about to be crucified, many of his followers, including Peter, His disciple, claimed that they didn't even know Jesus, but God used those same people to advance the Kingdom. I am sure they all had some consequences to deal with just from denying Christ, but that didn't stop them from being used by God.

In the beginning, we all know that Saul (Paul) was a full-fledged enemy of God and the people of God, and yet the Lord still saw fit to use Paul in a mighty, mighty big way. Paul became a martyr for Christ and he wrote several books in the New Testament. I am sure that there were consequences that had to be born by Paul as a result of his initial work against God. And I would hazard a guess that initially, forgiving himself had to be a major struggle. *"For I am the least of the apostles, who am not worthy to be called an apostle, because I persecuted the church of God." - 1 Corinthians 15:9.* Yet he was still used enormously.

Consequences are a direct result of disobedience, but again I say, if you let go and let God, he can still use you. T.D. Jakes once asked, *"Can you stand to be Blessed?"* That sounds like a crazy question with an easy answer, but in actuality it is not. Can you really stand to be blessed? Often times our actions say we can not.

He calls you, even when you aren't listening, when you don't know how to listen. The Father knows that the journey is going to be paved with trials, some self-inflicted, some not. Whatever the case, He is always ready to forgive and to help you heal so that He can use you to do His will. But you do play a role in this also. When you fall, get back up. Don't allow your disobedience to stop you from doing the work that you have been called to do. And all of us have been called to do something to advance the Kingdom. Not all on the same scale, but all equally important. Yes, we all have a job to do, so get up, wipe the dust off and be about the Lord's business!

STEP FIVE: *Disobedience does not disqualify you from God's use. Find out your purpose and seek His will for your life because He's still calling your name!*

Reflections: What are the first steps you need to take in your life in order to start being more obedient to Christ?

How will you go about changing your attitude toward an unequally yoked marriage?

What is your preferred method of praising God, in spite of your circumstance?

What are some things in your life that you can do without in order to purify your spirit, body, and mind?

What gifts has God given you which can be used in ministry to other Christians? What gifts has God given you that can be used in your very home?

In what ways has God used you in the past?

Discussion: God is still calling your name, He wants you to be a tool for his kingdom. That is why one of the most important things for you to do is to get plugged into a ministry so that you can be used. You are not worthless because of your disobedience.

The following poem is reflective of some of the many things one can experience and yet the Lord still calls us on to live purposeful and meaningful lives. After reading this poem, I suggest you go out and find a way to praise God. Sing along to some spiritual music, or just begin to tell God how wonderful He's been in your life. After all is said and done, I promise you will feel 100 times better!

Still Calling My Name

I've fallen more times that I care to remember,
than I care to even admit
How can someone who believes in every word of the
Gospel,
manage to constantly in sin to slip.

I've said and done unspeakable things,
the shame burns deeply within.
As a new believer, I thought I would always stand
strong—
nothing could make me stray or take my eyes off of
Him.

But I was a babe in the ways of Satan,
my faith had yet to be tried.
Before it was all over, I had been rebellious,
Disobedient, committed adultery, fornicated
and told countless lies.

Through all of this at times I managed to somehow
pray.
In my heart I believed that God was watching over me.
For every action there was chastening, for every sin
committed, I've paid a handsome fee.

Some of the consequences will last a lifetime, but at
least I am still here to tell the story.

That I am still breathing is high praise indeed, and to God I give all the glory.

For all that he has done and will do in my life to make me a better me.
His mercy is a blessing that I'm learning not to take for granted, because at anytime it could cease to be.

For reasons unknown I feel that God is not through with me yet. Since the day I accepted Him into my life, it hasn't been the same.
Through all the trials and temptations that I've been through, I still hear Him calling my name!

Chapter VI

Be Ye Not Unequally Yoked

*T*his last chapter is dedicated to all my sisters who are truly contemplating marriage to the wrong man. Do you want to know why he is wrong? I am sure you have great lines of defense to the contrary. I can hear them now, "He cooks for me. He cleans and, honey, when he kisses me, my whole body shivers. His body is rock hard and just the simple touch of his hand in mine makes me tingle all over. He's a good listener and he's good to my children. And I just know he's going to be a great provider." And because this walk is real, some of you are thinking, "He's the best lover I ever had." (This is a serious clue that you shouldn't even be talking about marriage, as you are already wrapped up in the sin of fornication.) My answer to all that is, "And"?!

Satan himself can give you all those things. But you wouldn't marry him, would you? On purpose? I think not, but if you marry an unsaved man knowingly, you are in fact, marrying the enemy, or at the very least, one of his minions.

Sounds a bit harsh, doesn't it? But the truth ain't always pretty and to marry a man that doesn't believe in Christ as you believe in Him, is a very dangerous game to play, or should I say, chance to take. If you are putting God first, why would you marry a man who doesn't put Him first in all things? To trust you and your children or future children to a man that is not seeking after God is tantamount to marrying Satan, in my humble opinion.

Ephesians 6:12
For we wrestle not against flesh and blood, but
against principalities, against powers, against the
rulers of darkness of this world, against spiritual
wickedness in high places."

Saints, we must realize that we are in a spiritual warfare today. Daily. Everyday. I mean now! And the fight is real. Why have it where you would be fighting twice as hard? Because you and your spouse will be on opposing sides. No matter how good his looks, works or upright his character, light and dark do not mix. Sometimes women (and men) can want a special someone in their lives so badly that they convince themselves that God sent unsaved people in their lives to marry, which is sad. We seem to convince ourselves that with all the other positive qualities the person possesses, that surely God would fix the rest, or maybe we could be the people to lead them to Christ. And to be honest, you very well could be, but it would not be after marriage, because the Lord would never lead you to be unequally yoked. The excuses we come up with are nothing more than justification of our behavior to feed our flesh.

Justification of sin is a good sign that we are either about to take a fall or have already done so. Because regardless of the person's unbelief, our flesh wants the marriage/relationship so much, that we lie to ourselves and truly believe on some level that God sent them. Others come up with equally poor justifications, "God knows I don't want to be alone," or this is one I have heard often, "God knows I have needs and I am only human." Now this God that people tend to speak of so casually and are close to being blasphemous about is Sovereign and to even say that He understands sinful desires to the extent that He condones them and turns a blind eye is just plain ignorant, and means that people don't know the God they claim to love and serve.

Ask yourself why a Sovereign God would send you an unsaved man. A man that does not believe in him who supposedly sent him? Just why would a God that loves you and has kept you for years suddenly decide that an unsaved man was worthy of entering in your holy temple, which is your body? He would not and could not do that, for then He would cease to be God. It is we who choose to make destructive, life-altering decisions. We choose our fleshly desires instead of seeking God's will. We make choices out of desperation and loneliness, acting as if God needs our help (because with the "male shortage" we are running out of options). We give Satan the opportunity to come into our lives for its very destruction. The enemy loves to fill our minds with that self-destructive way of thinking, so that we make choices that change the course of our lives negatively for years and years, sometimes unto death.

When we take our focus off of Jesus and we put it on man and/or our circumstances, we start to lose the battle. We may not lose the war, for nothing can separate us from the love, which is Christ Jesus, but we do lose some really important battles along the way. Battles that adversely affect our lives and possibly the lives of those we love for years to come.

Galatians 6:7-9 (NKJV)
"Do not be deceived, God is not mocked; for
whatever a man sows, that he will also reap. For
he who sows to the flesh; will of his flesh reap
corruption, but he who sows to the Spirit will of the
Spirit reap everlasting life. And let us not grow
weary while doing good, for in due season we shall
reap if we do not lose heart."

These verses tell us that if we live by worldly standards, those are the benefits that we will reap. This passage is letting saints know that we will get our just reward if we live according to the flesh. We want to have our cake and eat it too. We want to believe that we can live the life fantastic with very little, if any, consequences. We want to wallow in the pigsty and come up smelling like roses. NOT! Even after salvation, we still have that free will and it can still get us in trouble. Again, we won't lose our salvation, but it can help us to live a sort of hell here on earth.

These verses also tell us that we are not to grow weary in doing the right thing. For if we hold out, if we stand strong, as we do the will of the Father, that in the appointed time, we will reap the reward of life everlasting. So hold on, even when it's hard to do, and know that God is taking care of you and the Lord gives us no more than we can bear, even though it may not feel like it at the time.

Don't let your mouth right a check your rear can't cash by getting unequally yoked. Believe me, it will not matter how the Lord blesses materially or financially during your marriage, it will be a check that you were not emotionally or physically prepared to cash. Hear me on this—even living in a big house, with nice jobs or even the possible success of this book, does not change the fact that I live unequally yoked with all its corresponding consequences. And all the material things in the world do not bring peace to the _heart_ of my home. There is spiritual warfare going on between my husband and me that is constantly on simmer, prone to bouts of unexpected eruption. Be careful not to let material things cloud the real issue, which is the forfeiture of living in any semblance of peace except for maybe pockets of time. I can attest to that old saying, "If you lie down with the devil you will wake up in hell!"

If you have never taken the time to sit back and think about what it really means to be unequally yoked, I pray that you are at least now reconsidering the idea. No matter how in love you believe yourself to be, no matter how great any of his attributes, your heart and mind will hurt a lot less if you call off the wedding/relationship now! Read your Bible and pray on this matter diligently. Although, if the man is not saved, you already have your answer regarding marriage, and take it from experience, it's not worth it to try and change the answer or the man!

My pastor once preached a powerful sermon called "Christian Warfare," and in that sermon he broke it down to the nitty gritty and explained in depth the seriousness of the battle that we fight as Christians. The armor I spoke about in Chapter Three was taken from that same message. He explained that saints are called to war upon accepting Christ and in these latter days we had best pay attention and know our enemy. One of the first things we need to know is the enemy's goals, one of which is to ruin anything that gives God glory, one of which is the family. Total destruction of the family is at the top of the enemy's list. By doing this he can destroy testimonies, enslave us to sin, bringing us to his ultimate goal, which is to render us useless for God.

No, our salvation is intact, but what good are we to God when our families are falling apart at every turn. Take note, if the enemy can get you to believe that marrying an unsaved man "isn't all that bad," then he has accomplished much. To be unequally yoked is to put yourself in a position where the circumstances of your union could render you potentially useless for Christ. I didn't say *would*, I said *could* because you do not know if the consequences of said marriage are going to rock your foundation in such a fundamental way that you end up useless. Even if it renders you useless for only a season, you have given the enemy a victory of sorts and that is not what you want to do. That is why it is so important to put on the whole armor of God. Without it or Him, you can do nothing against the enemy but fail. As my pastor said, we cannot fight the Christian battle by human means, we need Jesus—especially when picking a spouse!

Think about it. A husband is to be the head of the family, getting his direction from Christ. So your spouse's being saved is of the utmost importance, because if he is not getting his direction from Christ, the only other alternative is the enemy, which can definitely bring about the destruction of the family. Do not forget, we are in a spiritual battle that is ongoing until Christ' return. Therefore being unequally yoked is definitely not a path that God's children need to take. Always remember, the enemy's ultimate goal is the ruination of anything that gives God any glory. If he can get you to begin your family on the wrong foot, it will make his job that much easier to accomplish. Remember, if there are children with this union, they can end up living in a home of constant turmoil, seen and unseen, maybe having to decide whether they prefer the darkness of one parent's life over the light of the other. It opens the door to even more influence from the enemy, as one is already living in the camp.

Please hear me when I say this, the Lord is not going to send you an unavailable man. In other words, the man God sends you will not be unsaved, jobless, homeless, separated or married, or even saved but jobless, homeless, separated or married. Those types of men are at the very least emotionally unavailable. If you diligently seek God's counsel and wait for an answer, the Lord will provide a man that is right for you or maybe He has another plan

73

for your life. It is not meant for all of us to be married. You may have been chosen to live for Christ totally without the distraction of a spouse, because the work he has in store for you is special.

Wanting a spouse is not a sin or wrong, but ignoring the Lord's will for your life in order to have a spouse is a sin, and could land you in a boatload of misery. That is why it is so important to seek out and to know the Lord's will for you life. If you seek him, you will find him.

32I want you to be free from the cares of this world. The man who is not married can spend his time working for the Lord and pleasing Him. 33The man who is married cares for the things of the world. He wants to please his wife. 34Married women and women who have never been married are different. The woman who has never been married can spend her time working for the Lord. She wants to please the Lord with her body and spirit. The woman who is married cares for the things of the world. She wants to please her husband. 35I am saying these things to help you. I am not trying to keep you from getting married. I want you to do what is best. You should work for Him without other things taking your time.
I Corinthians 7:32-35 (NLV)

2 Chronicles 15:2b (NKJV)
" If you seek Him, he will be found of you; but if
you forsake him,
he will forsake you."

We all have a choice. Will it be God or man? No matter which one you choose, there will be some consequences involved. The question is which consequences would you rather bear for an eternity? If you choose to be unequally yoked, do you forsake God, or do you forsake your spouse? Know this, you cannot serve two masters, as it says in *Matthew 6:24 – "No man can serve two masters: for either he will hate one, and love the other, or else he will hold to the one, and despise the other. Ye cannot serve God and mammom."*

I have only touched on some of the misery one can come to live with by marrying an unsaved man. There is one other truth that we need to be aware of and it is the possibility of your unsaved spouse turning your heart from the Lord. If the most wise King Solomon's heart could be turned from God, do not doubt that the same thing could happen to you (1 Kings 11:2-4)! *Unequal* is the key word here. Marrying out of the will of God will have its consequences.

It is my earnest prayer that what little I was able to convey will at least make one woman see that marrying a man who isn't saved, is an unwise choice when you consider the whole scheme of things.

I have listed a few things that you may want to consider before you get married—some thoughts and questions to ponder as you move towards a foundation that was established by God and a union that He takes very seriously, unto death.

1) Be in prayer about a potential mate before you consider marriage to anyone.

   - Make sure your heart and life are right before you make it a matter of prayer, so that you will know that you are hearing from God when you do.

75

- Think about what you really want in a mate, other than his being saved.
- Don't be afraid to be specific with God as you pray.

2) When you meet a man, be very sure of his salvation
   - Ask him his testimony—it should be given in detail.
   - Be cognizant of how he handles adversity.
   - Does he seek God in prayer in your presence? Do the two of you pray together?
   - Is he an active, tithing member of a church and is he spoken of highly among the brethren?
   - Is he saved, but currently living in a "back-slidden" state? Out of fellowship with God and has been for quite some time?

3) Have a long engagement, a year at the least.
   - Get to know your potential mate; communication is a must.
   - Trust your gut feelings, your own intuition. Is his walk real or does it seem contrived?
   - Does he make requests of you that are not biblical or make you uncomfortable?
   - Do not engage in premarital sex, and avoid situations that tempt you to do so. If you are doing so, STOP!

4) Always keep God first and He will direct your path.

- Read you Word daily.
- Pray without ceasing.

As I close this chapter I want you to ask yourself one important question. Could you handle knowing that your spouse died and went to hell? I pray this is something I will not face, but I believe it would be a hard pill to swallow. Not that we control who goes to heaven and who doesn't, but if you love your husband, and I can only assume that's true because you married him, then where his soul spends eternity can't help but matter to you.

As children of God, lost souls are our business. Telling people about Jesus and His gift of salvation is what we have been called to do. A burden for those who don't know Jesus is already something we feel. Accordingly, our husbands' dying and having not accepted Christ would hurt all the more, for our relationships with our spouses are more intimate. A loved one, such as a spouse, lost forever would probably be so much more painful. Therefore, consider carefully what you do, for disobedience has it own rewards.

These are just a few things that are worth some consideration, as you ponder marriage. Hopefully they will assist you in *not* becoming unequally yoked. I close with this chapter with a poem entitled the same.

Unequally Yoked

At night I barely sleep
My mind is focused on the man who made
Promises that he never intended to keep.

In the wee hours of the night I cry
As I come to terms with the fact that
On spiritual guidance from my
husband I cannot rely.

My heart aches so much, I sometimes feel
It's going to break
For I have made an unthinkable choice; I
Made a costly mistake.

"Till death do you part" is what the preacher said—
Those words constantly turn around over and
Over in my head!

His salvation may or may not happen—
This is another painful fact of life.
In ignorance, which is no excuse, I have chosen
To live with untold years of bickering and strife.

Truer words were never written or "spoke", as when
The Bible said, "Be ye not unequally yoked."

Final Thoughts

*I*t was not my goal to sound desolate or hopeless about my marriage or marriages that are unequally yoked. But neither did I want to sound like being unequally yoked is not a serious offense. It is. Listen. There is no fairy tale ending here. My husband is still not saved and the battles are still raging in my home. There is no peace. After 14 years, he is still not interested in accepting Christ or attending church.

What I had hoped to convey were the serious ramifications of disobedience in the area of marriage. When light and dark make a connection, sparks are going to fly! There is an abundance of friction that can never be controlled while my home serves two masters. I wanted to give some serious food for thought, and I can only pray that I have done so.

Lastly, I wanted the women of the world who are unequally yoked to know that they were not alone. There are tens of thousands of women out there living similar if not the same lives. I wanted them to know that with some refocusing, their lives can still be rich and rewarding. I wanted women to know that the plan God had for them is still out there. It is theirs to claim. We have to stop focusing on our husbands and what we feel they should or should not be doing, or are and aren't doing. Concentrate on God and the things of God and watch Him move in your life. Exercise some faith and know in your heart that *"faith is the substance of things hoped for, the evidence of things not seen"* (Hebrews 11:1), and that *without faith it is <u>impossible</u> to please him"* (Hebrews 11:6 – Emphasis added).

Life is all about choices. Will you make yours a matter of prayer and wait on God for the answer? It is your choice.

Choices

You meet.
You laugh.
You sigh.
Surely, this must be love.

You dream.
You marry.
You cry.
The honeymoon is over.

You fight.
You moan.
You lie.
Hard choices must now be made.

If in haste you sin.
In leisure you will repent.
Choices have their consequence.
When marrying in disobedience.

Biblical References

Some Scripture taken from the **New King James Version**. Copyright © 1982 by Thomas Nelson, Inc. Used by permission. All rights reserved."

Some Scripture taken from the **HOLY BIBLE, NEW INTERNATIONAL VERSION®**. Copyright © 1973, 1978, 1984 International Bible Society. Used by permission of Zondervan. All rights reserved.

Some Scripture taken from the **Holy Bible. New Living Translation** copyright © 1996 by Tyndale Charitable Trust. Used by permission of Tyndale House Publishers.

Some Scripture taken **New Life Version** from the Copyright © 1969 by Christian Literature International

Referenced Materials

The Hebrew - Greek Key Study Bible, *King James Version, 1984 and 1991, AMG Publishers, Chattanooga, TN 37422*

The Inspirational Study Bible by Max Lucado, *New King James Version*, 1995, Word Publishing, Dallas, London, Vancouver, Melbourne

Liberated Through Submission, *God's Design for Freedom in All Relationships*
P. B. Wilson, 1990, Harvest House Publishers, Eugene, Oregon 97402

Can You Stand to be Blessed? *Insights to Help You Survive the Peaks and Valleys*
T. D. Jakes, 1994, Treasure House, Shippensburg, PA 17257

Suggested Readings

Put the past behind you and give . . . The Gift of Forgiveness
Charles Stanley, 1987, Thomas Nelson, Inc., Nashville, Tennessee

Can You Stand to Be Blessed
Bishop T.D. Jakes, 1995, Treasure House.

Also, I would like to suggest **How to Handle Adversity** by Charles Stanley as additional reading.

Step One: How I Got Here

Step Two: The Importance of Forgiveness

Step Three: In the Valley

Step Four: Taming the Untamable

_____

_____

_____

_____

_____

_____

_____

_____

_____

_____

_____

_____

_____

_____

_____

_____

_____

_____

_____

_____

_____

_____

_____

_____

Step Five: Still Calling Your Name

For Those in Danger: The Warning Signs

About the Author

Kaye Edwards is a 40 year old mother of three residing in Southern Maryland. She works as a full-time Legal Secretary and operates a catering personnel service business that both she and her husband work on a part-time basis. Edwards has spent two years working on Unequally Yoked and prays for it to be a major impact on people's lives. Send comments to Kaye at:

P.O Box 682
Cheltenham, MD 20623

About the Publisher

Leeway Artisans, Inc. was established in 2003. The primary mission of Leeway Artisans is to provide Christian writers and artists of all kinds the opportunity to express their creativity through literature, photography, and art.

Leeway Artisans does not accept unsolicited manuscripts or artwork. We encourage all prospective artisans to submit their work electronically via info@leewayartisans.com with your work's title and brief description, your name and best means of contact. If you desire to send your manuscript, artwork, photography, or other material directly to us through mail, your envelope must have an identifiable from source that we can recognize. Any unsolicited envelope will be returned unopened or discarded if there is a lack of return address. Mailed submissions must include work title, description, proposal and author or originator of the work. Mail all submissions to:

Leeway Artisans
P.O. Box 1577
Laurel, MD 20707

And with all submissions, please do not send the original as they may get damaged or lost!

For more info visit www.leewayartisans.com

Check out other books from Leeway Artisans

One Giant Leap~love poems
A romantic lyric filled with passionate poems and vows thatspeak volumes on the importance of love and devotion in marriage. The perfect read for lovers of all ages!

"Mykle Lee is to poetry what Barry White is to song. 'One Giant Leap' into your arms Mykle...that would be a good way to spend time, or maybe I'll just read the book and dream." - Nikki Giovanni, author and poet

On Second South
Welcome to Second South Susquehanna, a dorm where Nerf battles abound, every inhabitant is a Buffy character, and the last thing on anybody's mind is studies. Robert Redding recounts the glory days of his junior year in this hilarious biography of college life at UMBC.

Laugh along with Robert as he recalls everything from procrastinated term papers and last minute cram sessions, to debates on the best lines from the *Matrix* and the impact of small group Bible study. You're **On Second South** - its college...or some form of it...from a Christian's perspective.

Pulp 7
A Sweet Deal...A Killer Calling...and A Man Inside...

All the way from Sweden comes one of the most thrilling writers known to Christian fiction. Michael Storm brings you three thrilling stories that will grip you with excitement and suspense and leave you craving more. Nothing is ever as it seems in the world of Pulp7!